# *Soprano*
# CLASSICAL CONTEST SOLOS
## With Companion Audio

CLASSICAL CONTEST SOLOS

ISBN 978-0-7935-7798-9

HAL•LEONARD®
CORPORATION
7777 W. BLUEMOUND RD. P.O. BOX 13819 MILWAUKEE, WI 53213

Visit Hal Leonard Online at
**www.halleonard.com**

# CONTENTS

*On the recordings:*
Sharon Garvey, soprano
Laura Ward, piano
Martha Gerhart, German and Italian language coach
Lelia Tenreyro, Spanish language coach

Recorded at WFMT studios, Chicago, 2/97
Larry Rock, engineer

The price of this publication includes access to companion recorded performances, piano accompaniments, and pronunciation lessons online, for download or streaming, using the unique code found on the title page. Visit **www.halleonard.com/mylibrary** and enter the access code.

# LEARNING A SONG

## *What is an art song?*

An art song is a composition, usually for voice and piano, of a classical nature. A composer chooses a poem or some prose and sets the words to music. This differs from popular songs, not only in musical style, but in artistic approach. For the genre of a popular song (anything from a song by George and Ira Gershwin to a song written by Sting) the words and music are written together. An art song is a musical reaction to an existing poem or text. The composer responds to the meaning of the words, as well as meanings that are implied, in a free, expressive manner. Art songs composed to poetry are a European tradition dating back to at least the Renaissance, and composers still continue to write new art songs today. The richest period for art song composition was in Germany, France and Italy during the nineteenth century. Many major composers created a large number of new art songs, for example, Schubert, Schumann, Fauré, Brahms, Mendelssohn, Wolf, Strauss, Bellini, Donaudy, and many others. Sometimes folksongs are arranged in an approach that gives them the sensibility of an art song intended for a singer and piano on the recital stage. Such is the case with Burleigh's settings of spirituals found in *Classical Contest Solos.*

## *Choosing a Song*

The most important factor in your success in performing any song, whether it be an art song, a pop song, or a theater song, is choosing a song that is suitable for your voice. Deciding which song to sing will necessitate some experimentation when you are just beginning to study voice. Choose a song that you like. Make certain that the vocal range is reasonable for you. There probably will be some vocal challenges for you, and that is as it should be. Don't make the mistake of choosing a song that is so difficult for you that it becomes a burden, and is something that you ultimately cannot sing at your best. The songs in *Classical Contest Solos* vary some in vocal difficulty, but all should be reasonable for student singers. Nevertheless, they pose different challenges.

## *The Poem*

Always remember that in art song the words came first. The composer's song wouldn't exist without the poet's original words, sometimes written hundreds of years before the song was composed. You will do well to begin your study of a song by first pondering the words. What do they mean? Is there an implied character that says the words? (Sometimes this is true, but not always.) What is implied, but left unsaid? Is there something that has happened before the poem begins? You will have to use your imagination and insight to arrive at your own conclusions. Is the language of the poem stylized in some way, because of the period in which it was written, or the nationality of the author, or because the author chose deliberately to say things in a particular way? What are the most important words in the poem? If you have difficulty understanding a poem you might ask for help from someone experienced in poetry and literature, an English teacher, for example.

As you ponder the poem's meaning you should recite the words aloud. An actor learning a part would naturally say the words aloud many times, experimenting with different inflections and stresses. A singer should work in the same way, considering the words of the song over and over from many different points of view. After you learn the music, which we will soon address, the crucial next step is to attempt to discover what the *composer* felt the poem is about, and how his/her setting of the words to music reveals the meaning. You may discover that the composer has interpreted the words in a way different from anything you had previously considered.

## *Songs in a Foreign Language*

All of the comments in the section above also apply to a song for which the words are in Italian, German, Spanish, or any language other than English. Yet there is an obvious added challenge: You must learn to correctly pronounce a poem in a language that you probably do not speak. Classical singers the world over, particularly in the United States, learn early on that they must be proficient in singing in the major European languages. This does not mean that they all can speak these languages fluently.

Why do we not just translate art songs originally written in German, Italian, Spanish, French, or any other language into English? The answer is that the original poem is so intricately a part of the music that changing the words in any way would be the same as altering the music. It is also very difficult, if not impossible, to adequately translate a poem into another language and retain the subtleties of meanings originally intended. The English translations in *Classical Contest Solos* are for comprehension and study, but they are not designed to be sung. In opera it may make sense sometimes to translate the words for an audience sitting in the theater trying to follow a plot. But art song is a far more intimate kind of composition. It is generally accepted internationally that, with rare exceptions, an art song always should be performed in the original language.

The recorded pronunciation lessons on the companion audio will aid you greatly in learning how to pronounce the words to a poem in a foreign language. This study must be very meticulous. Do not just approximate the sounds you hear by the recorded teacher. Work at exactly imitating the vowels and consonants. Once you can accurately pronounce the text of the poem phonetically, practice speaking it many times until it becomes a fluent expression. Put the poems in your own words to discover the meanings. Your goal is for those who hear you sing the song to believe that you are a fluent, native speaker of the language you sing. Does that sound impossible? It isn't, with hard, intelligent work.

## *Learning the Melody and Rhythms*

After you have studied the words as described above, which may take several days of study, it is time to learn the musical notes. If you are capable of playing an instrument, you will do best to play a phrase, then sing it as you study the notes. Repeat the phrase as many times as is necessary for you to feel you know all the notes and rhythms correctly. If you do not play an instrument, and many singers do not, you may want to consider taking piano lessons. This will help enormously. In the meantime, you will have to ask someone to play the melody notes for you. Listen carefully to the pitches and rhythms, and practice them regularly until you know them completely. It is very important that you also learn how many beats of rest there are whenever you are not singing. Many singers fail to study rests carefully, and the result is that they enter early with a vocal phrase, or are late in coming in at the correct spot.

The companion recording can help you to learn a song. Listen carefully to the singer on the recording, all the while following along, studying the notes on the page. You can stop the recording and study a phrase at a time like this. One word of caution: While it may be very useful for you to use the recording to learn the notes, you will not want to imitate every interpretive nuance as done by the recorded singer. You will want to study the song thoroughly so that you can come up with your own interpretation.

## *Practice*

After you have studied the words and learned the melody and rhythms, you must practice the song regularly, probably meaning almost every single day. Remember that classical singing is not just about getting the pronunciation, notes and rhythms right. You must work on your singing, learning how to produce the most beautiful and natural sound possible, smoothly moving from one note to the next. This is best accomplished with the guidance of a voice teacher. However, you might ask your choral director for help, or your church choir director. Practice sessions should begin with warm-ups. Remember that beautiful classical singing is never strained. Do not try to make more sound than is naturally comfortable. Your aim is a healthy, open sound that is supported by good breathing. The ultimate aim is to have no tension in your jaw, your throat, your face, or anywhere else in your body as you sing. A solid, low breath from the diaphragm (in the abdomen) is absolutely necessary, not a high, shallow breath that comes from your chest. The recorded accompaniments to this volume will help you greatly in your practice. However, when you perform a song with a live pianist you are free to take a different tempo than the one on the recording.

## *Memorizing*

All songs that solo singers present in a performance with piano should be memorized. College voice majors sing a whole recital from memory. Professional artists sing a repertoire of many opera roles in several languages, all from memory. If you are having difficulty memorizing a song, it is probably because you haven't studied it long enough or carefully enough.

## *Performing*

You should find ways to get your nerves under control. Practice "performing" for your friends or family before you sing for judges or an audience. You should know the music *extremely well*. All too often students quickly learn a song the week before a performance, then don't quite understand when things don't go smoothly. You should know something very well several weeks before the performance. Only then will you be able to express yourself as an emerging artist, communicating something from within you. In the best situation you will perform with a pianist, not with the recorded practice accompaniment.

# Didn't My Lord Deliver Daniel

**HARRY T. BURLEIGH** (1866-1949)

African-American composer and arranger Harry Thacker Burleigh was born in Erie, Pennsylvania in 1866, one year after the end of the Civil War. His grandfather had been a slave who was "let go" by his slaveholders when he became blind. Upon graduating from high school, Burleigh won a scholarship to study at the National Conservatory of Music in New York, and was able to make the move with the help of many donations from contributors in his home town of Erie. While at the conservatory he was heavily influenced by the school's director, composer and conductor Antonín Dvořák. Like many musicians, Burleigh found it difficult to make a living performing and composing. His principal employment throughout most of his adult life was as a music editor at the New York office of the Italian music publisher Ricordi. He spent his summers traveling to Milan to work at the home office. Burleigh composed some 265 vocal pieces, and is credited with a collection of African-American minstrel melodies. He was a prominent baritone soloist in New York, first at St. George's Church, then for 25 years at Temple Emanuel-El. Burleigh also regulary sang in recital. He did ground-breaking work with his documentation and arrangements of 187 spirituals for choir. Burleigh was also one of the first to take this music of African-American heritage into the concert hall in arrangements for solo voice and piano. He had learned many spirituals as a child, listening to his grandfather sing. Burleigh was an excellent and respected vocal coach who worked with famous singers such as Enrico Caruso, Marian Anderson and Paul Robeson. He was a founding member of ASCAP. Among the honors bestowed on Harry Burleigh were an honorary master's degree from Atlanta University, an honorary Doctor of Music degree from Harvard University, and in 1917 the Spingarn Medal was awarded to him by the N.A.A.C.P., citing him for the highest achievement by an African-American for the year 1916.

**THOUGHTS ABOUT THE SONG ...**

Spirituals, predominantly the songs of African-American slaves, are an important part of our American musical heritage. Though they have their roots with African-Americans, experts on spirituals maintain that today they are music for all singers of all races. There are several types of spirituals. Many are slow and soulful, dreaming of a better life after death. Some are a rowdy good time. Others are based on Bible stories, more of a forthright declaration of faith necessary for getting through the present. "Didn't My Lord Deliver Daniel" is a rhythmic spiritual, but one couldn't call this merely a "good time" song. It has a desperation about it, as if the singer is trying to bolster her faith and the faith of her listeners. At the same time, she is telling the story of Daniel in a very dramatic and captivating way. Keep this song rhythmic and moving along. Don't slow down at all (until the big *ritard.* at the end). While it's important to get the rhythms and syncopations exactly right, one wouldn't want to sing this song in a straight-laced classical manner. Loosen up! A singer may use as much dialect in pronunciation of the words as is comfortable for this style. Some singers will feel perfectly comfortable using a full-fledged southern African-American dialect. Others will feel more comfortable staying more closely to standard American English pronunciation.

**PRONUNCIATION TIP**

Burleigh [**burr**-lee]

# Didn't My Lord Deliver Daniel

story from
the Book of Daniel
chapter 6

African-American Spiritual
original arrangement by
Harry T. Burleigh
adapted by Richard Walters

ev - 'ry poor soul __ that nev - er did pray __ will be glad to pray __ that day. Did - n't

my Lord de - liv - er Dan - iel, __ de - liv - er Dan - iel, __ de - liv - er Dan - iel? __ Did - n't

my Lord de - liv - er Dan - iel, __ and why not ev - er - y man? I

set my foot on the Gos - pel ship, and the ship it be - gin __ to __ sail. It

land - ed me o - ver on Ca - naan's shore, and I'll nev - er come back an - y -

more. My Lord de - liv - er Dan - iel, He de -

liv - er Dan - iel, He de - liv - er Dan - iel. Did - n't my Lord de - liv - er

Dan - iel, and why not ev - er - y man?

# Do not go, my love

**RICHARD HAGEMAN** (1882-1966)

By the time Richard Hageman was only sixteen years old he was coaching singers at the Netherlands Opera Company. He received his first music lessons from his father, who taught at the New Music Institute in Amsterdam and the Conservatory of Brussels. He worked as an accompanist to singer Mathilde Marchesi in Paris, and immigrated to the United States in 1906 as the accompanist of Yvette Guilbert. He became a conductor at the Metropolitan Opera in New York in 1908, staying until 1922. In 1922 and 1923 he worked with the Civic Opera in Chicago, and later with the Los Angeles Grand Opera. He served as conductor of the Fairmont Symphony Orchestra in Philadelphia and was head of the opera department at the Curtis Institute of Music. Hageman's opera *Caponsacchi* was performed at the Metropolitan Opera in 1937. He also wrote various concert dramas and a large number of art songs and popular songs. As of 1940, Hageman could be found in Hollywood where he wrote the score and various songs *for This Woman Is Mine* (1940) and *Wagon Master* (1950). He provided the score for the film *Angel and the Badman* (1946), and appeared in the cast of the Mario Lanza films *The Great Caruso* (1951), *New Orleans* (1947), and *Toast of New Orleans* (1950).

**SIR RABINDRANATH TAGORE** (1861-1941)

Tagore was an Indian poet, playwright, novelist, musician and philosopher who wrote principally in Bengali, then translating his own writings into English. He only wrote one poem originally in English. He was the most important Indian writer of his time. He was born in Calcutta. Tagore was educated in England and traveled there often. He is cited as writing the first modern novel by an Indian author, *Binodini*. The poet won the Nobel Prize in 1913 for his collection of poems *Gitanjali*. Throughout his life and works Tagore was interested in the relationship between a European education and Eastern philosophy. He founded a university in India with that aim. He was knighted by the British in 1917 (India was under British rule at the time), but resigned his knighthood in 1919 in protest against British policy in India. Like all other leaders in India at the time, he strongly favored self-rule.

**THOUGHTS ABOUT THE SONG ...**

This American art song, first published in 1917, is the dramatic plea of the poet (singer) at the deathbed of a loved one. She has been restless for days, barely sleeping at all, waiting by the bed of her dying beloved. In the words "do not go, my love without asking my leave" she is desparately saying: please don't die while I'm not here by your side, close to you. She tells us how she fears she will "lose you while I am sleeping." After she states "Is it a dream?", we hear the music shift into a different mood. In the words "Could I but entangle your feet with my heart, and hold them fast to my breast," she states her wish to hold onto her beloved. Then as the music returns to the beginning of the song, we hear that she again faces the reality of the imminent death at hand. From a vocal point of view you will need to experiment with just the right vowel sound on the high F-sharp on the word "leave" in order to make the note as beautiful as possible. The same vowel occurs on the other high note, on the word "dream." Your aim is a free sound, easily produced, without tension.

**PRONUNCIATION TIPS**

Richard Hageman [**hah**-guh-mun]
Sir Rabindranath [rah-bin-**drah**-nath] Tagore [tah-**gor**]

# Do not go, my love

poem by
Sir Rabindranath Tagore

music by
Richard Hageman

when I am sleep - ing.

Do not go, my love,

with - out ask - ing my leave.

**Più mosso**

I start up and

stretch my hands _____ to touch you.

I ask my - self, "Is it a

dream?" _____

**Tempo I Più mosso**

Could I but en - tan - gle your feet

# I Attempt from Love's Sickness to Fly

**HENRY PURCELL** (1659-1695)

From the time of John Dowland to the notable figures of the 20th century, Henry Purcell stands alone as the greatest British composer. Like many of his contemporaries, he came from a musical family. (His brother Daniel was also a composer.) Purcell was a chorister at the Chapel Royal in London at the age of ten. In 1673 he left this position and began his study with composer John Blow, succeeding him in 1679 as organist at Westminster Abbey. Purcell became very interested in writing theatre music, and composed incidental music and songs for over 50 dramatic works. The song "I Attempt from Love's Sickness to Fly" was written to be sung in a musical play entitled *The Indian Queen. Dido and Aeneas* (1689), the first true opera in the English language, was his only through-composed opera. Purcell served in royal appointments throughout his short life. In 1685 King James II named him the Royal Harpsichordist. Despite these court appointments, Purcell relied on his theatre work for much of his income, as well as for his creative fulfillment. He also composed a large amount of church music, including music for the funeral of Queen Mary in 1694. The same music was performed at his own funeral one year later.

**THOUGHTS ABOUT THE SONG...**

This is one of the most often heard of Purcell's songs, and is a favorite of voice teachers assigning songs to student singers. This song is a graceful minuet, yet it expresses emotions of someone who has been hurt by loving someone, and that love was not returned. The artfulness in singing this song is to retain both of those opposing ideas: gracefulness and sincere despair. This is stylized language, as is all poetry. The nature of art is to express an emotion in a way different from the prose of everyday speech. In everyday language the words of the songs might be paraphrased as follows.

| *original* | *paraphrase in modern language* |
|---|---|
| I attempt from love's sickness to fly in vain, | I try not to fall in love, |
| Since I am myself my own fever and pain. | but I can't help myself. |
| | |
| No more now, fond heart, | My dear heart |
| with pride no more swell, | can't swell with pride and confidence |
| Thou canst not raise forces enough to rebel. | because it isn't strong enough to resist. |
| | |
| For Love has more power and less mercy than fate | [this phrase is clear in modern English] |
| To make us seek ruin and on those that hate. | to make us love those that scorn us. |

One very interesting and important thing to realize is that in musical form the song is a rondo. A rondo is a type of musical piece that has a theme section that continues to be stated, but with other musical material interspersed. For instance, the music on the first page of the song is the rondo theme, which we will label as Section A for purposes of discussion. The music that begins at the words "No more now" we will label Section B. On page three of the song we have another section of different music that we haven't previously heard, beginning at the words "For love has more power." This we'll label Section C. Using the sections as cited above, the musical form for this song is AA(the repeat)BACAA. When these rondo themes repeat (A) it is in the style of this period to find little ways to vary the melody slightly. The smaller sized notes in the score are the editor's suggestions for such ornamentation. The soprano on the recording chose slightly different melodic variations. If any of the ornamentation suggested in the music (the smaller sized notes) is difficult for you, or doesn't flatter you, then you should change it to something that does work for you. Or it is perfectly acceptable to sing the melody as is, without ornamentation.

**PRONUNCIATION TIPS**

Henry Purcell [**pur**-sull, *not* pur-**sell**]

# I Attempt from Love's Sickness to Fly

Henry Purcell
1695

[Minuet tempo]

18

more now, no more now, fond ___ heart, with pride no more

swell, Thou canst not ___ raise ___ for - ces, thou canst not ___ raise ___

for - ces e - nough to re - bel. I at - tempt from Love's ___

sick - ness to fly _____ in ___ vain. Since I am my -

* optional melodic ornamentation by the editors
** appoggiatura possible

self my own fe - ver, since I am my - self my own fe - ver \_ and \_

pain. For Love has more \_ power and less mer - cy than fate. To

make us \_ seek \_ ru - in. to \_ make \_ us \_ seek \_ ru - in and \_ on those \_ that \_

hate. I at - tempt from Love's \_ sick - ness to fly _____ in \_

# El tra la la y el punteado

| El tra la la y el punteado | *The tra-la-la and the guitar-plucking* |
| --- | --- |

Es en balde, majo mío,  
Que sigas hablando,  
Porque hay cosas que contesto  
Yo siempre cantando.  
Por más que preguntes tanto,  
En mi no causas quebranto,  
Ni yo he de salir de mi canto.

*It is useless, my beloved,*  
*to continue talking,*  
*for there are things to which I answer*  
*always in song.*  
*Even with all your questioning,*  
*you will not make me weaken,*  
*neither will I stop singing.*

## ENRIQUE GRANADOS  (1867-1916)

Perhaps if Enrique Granados' opera *Goyescas* had not been such a hit at its Metropolitan Opera premiere on January 28, 1916, he would have lived to be an old man.  Instead, President Woodrow Wilson invited the Spanish composer for a visit at the White House.  Granados and his wife travelled from New York to Washington, knowing that they would miss their planned voyage back to Spain.  When the visit was over they instead boarded the S.S. Sussex, which sailed for Britain, and planned to book passage from there to Spain.  A German submarine changed those plans, sinking the S.S. Sussex in the British Channel. Granados was rescued by a lifeboat, but saw his wife struggling to stay afloat in the sea. He jumped in to save her. Sadly, both he and his wife drowned. Before he found success as a composer, Granados made his living in Spain, playing piano in various restaurants and giving private concerts.  He wrote four operas that were performed in Barcelona. The operas attracted little attention, but a series of piano pieces entitled *Goyescas*, inspired by etchings and paintings of the artist Goya, caught the public's attention.  Written in 1911, the piano pieces became the basis for his opera by the same name. Just a few months before his death, thrilled by the success of *Goyescas*, he wrote to a friend, "I have a whole world of ideas...I am only now starting my work."

## THOUGHTS ABOUT THE SONG...

A young woman is addressing her boyfriend. He has been courting her, but she has tired of his words. She doesn't want to answer his romantic pleas directly, maybe for many reasons. (Perhaps she has another boyfriend, and she doesn't want to commit to this one. Or maybe she doesn't know how she feels about him, but wants to continue to see him. It could be that she just wants to tease him. Perhaps he's accusing her of being unfaithful to him. You can use your imagination to come up with your own ideas about her motivation.) One interpretation would be as follows: She begins to play the guitar, or she hears a guitar playing nearby. She is a singer, and loves more than anything to sing. She flirtatiously says to her boyfriend (paraphrased): You can talk to me all you want, but I will not give you an answer. I will sing my tra-la-la, have a good time, and you can make what you want of it. This is a playful song, and you should be joyful and flirtatious in your performance. If Spanish is not your principal language you will want to work diligently on the correct pronunciation of the words, using the recorded lesson on the companion audio. Speak the words over and over until they become comfortable and fluent. This may take several days work. Only then, when you feel so at ease with the words that you can express yourself through them, should you attempt to sing them.

## PRONUNCIATION TIP

Enrique [en-**ree**-kay] Granados [grah-**nah**-dohs]

# El tra la la y el punteado

poem by
Fernando Periquet

music by
Enrique Granados

**Allegro**

Es

en bal - de ma - jo mi - o que si - gas ha - blan - do, por que hay co - sas que con-

*p (tempo primo on repeat)*

*rit.* *2nd time*

tes - to yo siem - pre can - tan - do. Tra la la la la la la la la la la la la

**To Coda**

la la la la la la.

*(a little slower)*

Por mas que pre - gun - tes tan - to. Tra la la la la la;

la; en ___ mi no cau - sas que - bran - to ni yo he de sa - lir de mi can - to

*(rit.)*

*(a tempo)*

la la la la la la la.

**D.S. al Coda**

Es -

**CODA**

# Se tu m'ami

**Se tu m'ami**                     *If you love me*

| | |
|---|---|
| Se tu m'ami | *If you love me,* |
| se tu sospiri sol per me, | *if you sigh only for me* |
| gentil pastor, | *gentle shepherd,* |
| ho dolor de' tuoi martiri, | *I am sorry for your suffering,* |
| ho diletto del tuo amor. | *I take pleasure in your love.* |
| Ma se pensi che soletto | *But if you think that you alone* |
| io ti debba riamar, | *I should love in return,* |
| pastorello, sei soggetto | *little shepherd, you are subject* |
| facilmente a t'ingannar. | *easily fooling yourself.* |
| Bella rosa porporina | *A beautiful red rose* |
| oggi Silvio sceglierà; | *today Silvio will choose;* |
| con la scusa della spina | *with the excuse of its thorn* |
| doman poi la sprezzerà. | *tomorrow, then, he will reject it.* |
| Ma degli uomini il consiglio | *But the advice of men* |
| io per me non seguirò. | *I, myself, will not follow.* |
| Non perché mi piace il giglio | *Just because the lily pleases me* |
| gli altri fiori sprezzerò. | *I will not reject the other flowers.* |

**ALESSANDRO PARISOTTI** (1853-1913), composer and musicologist, might have been forgotten by history were it not for his work on a collection of old arias entitled *Arie antiche 1600-1800,* published by Ricordi. His work (published in America in the very commonly used G. Schirmer *edition 24 Italian Songs and Arias of the 17th and 18th Centuries*) is a collection of short arias that remains an international staple of a classical singers'study. These arias are from long forgotten operas. At the time it was common to substitute arias into operas, so they often had little specifically to do with a character or plot. Parisotti spent his life in Rome, where he composed a wealth of sacred music and served as secretary of the Accademia di Santa Cecilia. In the 1880s he researched the old Italian music of the 17th and 18th centuries. Up until that time, the Italian music of the baroque period was almost completely unknown to 19th century singers. Curiously, Parisotti included one of his own original compositions set to a text by Rolli, an 18th century Italian poet, in the Ricordi publication, "Se tu m'ami," crediting it to Giovanni Pergolesi (1710-1736). Why did Parisotti falsely credit Pergolesi in the publication? Perhaps he felt that it would be better received under the name of an old master, or perhaps he was merely timid in presenting it as his own. The truth is likely to remain a mystery. The important thing is that this is a beautiful song, expertly composed in an 18th century Italian style.

## THOUGHTS ABOUT THE SONG...

The pastoral imagery of a love scene between a shepherd and a shepherdess is traditional in European literature, poetry, opera and painting. Usually, as in this case, the shepherdess is flirtatious and fickle. She teases the shepherd who loves her, though she feels a bit sorry for him. She declares that she doesn't want to belong to any one suitor. Using the simile of a rose, she describes how a man, Silvio, for instance, likes a girl one day, then finds an excuse tomorrow to reject her. She wants that kind of freedom, but she doesn't want to be like a man. Instead, she implies that just because she likes one fellow, it doesn't mean that she can't like another as well. Though the song is in a minor key, it is certainly not at all sad. It is playful, and should be sung that way. Work with the pronunciation lesson on the companion audio to perfect your Italian pronunciation, speaking the words over and over until they are completely comfortable and fluent.

## PRONUNCIATION TIPS

Alessandro [ah-lehs-**sahn**-droh] Parisotti [pah-ree-**sot**-tee - pronounce the "o" as in the word "of"]

# Se tu m'ami

poem by
Paolo Antonio Rolli

music by
Alessandro Parisotti

Se tu m'a - mi, __ se tu so - spi - ri Sol __ per me, __ gen - til __ pa - stor, Ho do - lor de' tuoi mar - ti - ri, Ho di - let - to del tuo a - mor, __ Ma __ se pen - si che __ so - let - to Io __ ti __ deb - ba ri - a - mar, Pa - sto - rel - lo, sei sog - get - to

cresc. un poco

Io per me non se-gui-rò. Non per-chè mi pia-ce il gi-glio Gli al-tri fio-ri

sprez - ze - rò.

Se tu m'a - mi, se tu so-spi-ri Sol per

me, gen-til pa - stor, Ho do-lor de' tuoi mar-ti-ri,

Ho di - let - to del tuo a - mor, ___ Ma se pen - si, che ___ so - let - to

Io ___ ti ___ deb - ba ri ___ a - mar. Pa - sto - rel - lo, sei sog - get - to

Fa - cil - men - te a t'in - gan - nar, Pa - sto - rel - lo, sei sog - get - to

Fa - cil - men - te a t'in - gan - nar, Fa - cil - men - te a t'in - gan - nar.

# It Was a Lover and His Lass

**THOMAS MORLEY** (c. 1557-1602)

Like many professional English musicians of the Renaissance and Baroque, composer Thomas Morley began his musical life as a chorister, singing at St. Paul's Cathedral in London. He was an early pupil of William Byrd and received his music degree from Oxford University in 1588. At about the same time, he became the organist at St. Giles' Church in London. In 1589 he was appointed organist at St. Paul's Cathedral, and in 1592 he was granted the honorary title of Gentleman of the Chapel Royal. Morley lived in the same parish as Shakespeare, and at times composed music for Shakespeare plays. Morley was an excellent music teacher, and wrote a treatise *A Plaine and Easie Introduction to Practicall Musicke*, published in 1597 (note the old English spellings). He was famous in his day for writing madrigals, and helped compile *The Triumphs of Oriana* (1601), a collection of madrigals by various composers in praise of Queen Elizabeth. Morley also composed church music in English and Latin, instrumental pieces, and keyboard pieces. "It Was a Lover and His Lass" is typical of a part-song of the period. Like other pieces of its type, it was performed as a SATB choral piece, or as a solo song with the singer taking the top line and instruments playing the other parts as an accompaniment.

**THOUGHTS ABOUT THE SONG...**

This lively song is typical of the happy songs of the English Renaissance. It is about two rural young people in love in the springtime. A common poetic idea of shepherd and shepherdess was a convention of the time. Why? Because carefree shepherds were not bound by the formal social conventions and pretensions of London society, and in the peace and beauty of the countryside they could express themselves freely. Of course, the poets and musicians who perpetuated the myth of the happy shepherds were themselves city people who had no idea how hard a shepherd's life really is!

"With a hey and a ho and hey nonie no" is a common nonsense phrase that expresses joy, similar to "fa la la." The word "nonie" probably is related in the word "nonsense." There are more musical nonsense words, this time expressing bird sounds, in "hey ding-a-ding-a-ding."

This song needs crisp, accurate rhythm for it to sparkle. It would not be a bad idea to work on a light (not overdone) British accent for this very English music. The small sized notes in the music are suggestions for melodic ornamentation that may be sung on any verse after the first one. You may elect not to sing these, or to sing slightly different ornamentation of your own invention.

For our recording, we chose to present only two verses of the song. You might choose to do the same for a performance.

# It Was a Lover and His Lass

words from As You Like It,
William Shakespeare

Thomas Morley

[Lively]

1. It was a lov-er and his lass,
2. Be - tween the a - cres of the rye,
3. This car - ol they be - gan that hour,
4. Then, pret - ty lov - ers, take the time,

With a hey, and a ho, and a hey non-ie no, and a hey _____ non-ie non-ie no,

That o'er the green corn - field did pass
These pret - ty coun - try fools did lie
How that life was but a flow'r
For love is crown - ed with the prime

In spring - time, in spring - time, in spring - time, The on - ly pret - ty ring - time, When

*The editors' optional melodic ornamentation is for verse 3 or 4.*

# Lachen und Weinen

**Lachen und Weinen**

Lachen und Weinen zu jeglicher Stunde
ruht bei der Lieb auf so mancherlei
Morgens lacht' ich vor Lust,
und warum ich nun weine
bei des Abendes Scheine,
ist mir seb' nicht bewusst.

Weinen und Lachen zu jeglicher Stunde
ruht bei der Lieb auf so mancherlei Grunde.
Abends weint's ich vor Schmerz;
und warum du erwachen kannst
am Morgen mit Lachen,
muss ich dich fragen, o Herz.

*Laughing and crying*

*Laughing and crying at every hour
caused in love by so many things.
At morning light I laughed for joy,
and why I now weep
in the evening's glow,
I myself do not know.*

*Crying and laughing at every hour
caused in love by so many things.
In the evening I wept with sorrow;
and why you can awaken
in the morning with laughter,
must I ask you, oh heart.*

## FRANZ SCHUBERT (1797-1828)

The work of the great Austrian composer Franz Schubert was largely overlooked during his short lifetime. It was not until some 50 years after his death that one of his symphonies was finally published. Schubert was the son of a Viennese schoolmaster. Of his ten siblings, only Franz and two others would survive to adulthood. Despite the extraordinary musical ability Schubert showed as a child, he was expected to follow in his father's profession. Schubert was educated at the Imperial and Royal Seminary on a music scholarship, singing in the choir in return for free tuition, room and board. He remained in the Chapel School until his voice changed in 1813, by which time his first symphony was already completed. Schubert taught at his father's school for two years, trading the security of a job for the freedom to compose. He wrote music in every free moment, at a feverish pace, as he would for the rest of his life. In the year 1815 alone, he wrote 144 songs, two masses, two symphonies, one opera, several choral works, four operettas and a variety of piano pieces. Yet Schubert would only get the briefest taste of success. After years of crushing poverty and poor reviews for his stage works, a successful, all-Schubert concert was given on March 26, 1828. He died seven months later. In his 31 years, Schubert composed more than 600 songs, eight symphonies, in addition to chamber music, piano pieces, operas, operettas and choral music. Schubert was buried as near to his idol, Beethoven, as was possible.

## THOUGHTS ABOUT THE SONG ...

First, you must study the German pronunciation very carefully, working with the companion recording. It is crucial for a successful performance of any Lied (the term for a German art song). It may take several days of work before you feel comfortable with the German words. Listen very carefully to the teacher on the recording and match her pronunciation exactly. Only after you feel you can fluently speak the words should you attempt to sing them. Don't be afraid to roll your R's! This is a song of a teenage girl who is in love for the first time in her life. She doesn't understand her feelings. Why is she delirious with joy one minute, and crying her eyes out the next minute? The powerful feeling of love is playing tricks with her emotions, and it's such a new experience to her that she doesn't understand what's happening. Have you ever felt like this? If so, you might look back on it and laugh at yourself for being such a wreck about something. So too, this song, though sincere, creates a subtle, playful comic effect.

## PRONUNCIATION TIPS

Franz [frahnz] Schubert [**shoo**-behrt]
Friedrich [**free**-drick] Rückert [**ruk**-erht - the "u" vowel is a combination of these vowel sounds: "put" and "pit"]

# Lachen und Weinen

poem by
Friedrich Rückert

music by
Franz Schubert

La - chen und Wei - nen zu jeg - li - cher Stun - de ruht _ bei der

Lieb _ auf so man - cher - lei Grun - de. Mor - gens lacht' ich vor Lust, _____

_ und wa - rum ich nun wei - ne bei des

A - bends weint' ich vor Schmerz; _____ und wa - rum du er -

wachen kannst am Mor - gen mit La - chen, muß ich dich fra - gen, o Herz, muß ich dich

fra - gen, o Herz.

# Nel cor più non mi sento

| **Nel cor più non mi sento** | ***In my heart I no longer feel*** |
|---|---|
| Nel cor più non mi sento | *In my heart I no longer feel* |
| brillar la gioventù; | *the sparkle of youth;* |
| cagion del mio tormento, | *the cause of my torment,* |
| amor, sei colpa tu. | *love, is your fault.* |
| Mi pizzichi, mi stuzzichi, | *You pinch me, you excite me,* |
| Mi pungichi, mi mastichi; | *you prick me, you bite me,* |
| che cosa è questo ahimè? | *what thing is this, alas?* |
| Pietà! | *Pity me!* |
| Amore è un certo che | *Love is a certain something* |
| che disperar mi fa. | *which makes me delirious.* |

**GIOVANNI PAISIELLO** (1740-1816)

The son of an Italian veterinarian, Giovanni Paisiello was a tremendously successful composer of comic operas. As a student, he focused his energy on sacred music, writing his first secular dramatic work just before he left school. In 1776 he was invited to serve as *maestro di cappella* in the Russian court of Empress Catherine II. His contract to Catherine's court was extended twice. But when Paisiello was offered a post as composer of dramatic music in Naples, he used his wife's ill health as an excuse to return to Italy despite his contractual obligations. Catherine, not wanting to lose him, gave him a year's paid leave, but Paisiello never returned to Russia. Once in Italy, he was caught up for a time in the winds of political change, finding himself in favor when the Republicans came to power and then out of favor when the Royalists took control. He eventually was appointed to various lofty musical posts, losing all but one of them in the political upheavals of 1815. Paisiello composed over 90 operas, and was particularly highly successful in the realm of comic operas. In addition he wrote several masses and oratorios as well as twelve symphonies, six harpsichord concertos and various chamber pieces.

**THOUGHTS ABOUT THE SONG...**

This little aria is from an obscure opera of 1789 entitled *L'Amor contrastato* (The Opposing Love). It is sung by a young woman who is bewildered at being in love. Her boyfriend teases her, tickles her, and according to the lyrics, he even bites her! (We can assume that it's a playful little nibble, not an injury-causing bite!) Maybe she's never had a man's affection and attention before, and it's driving her crazy with confusion. It's an amusing song. It needs personality, sparkle, and maybe a bit of cuteness. Practice your Italian pronunciation carefully, speaking the words many, many times until they become fluent. Listen to the companion recording for a pronunciation lesson. It will take several sessions of practice at the words to get them comfortable enough so that you feel you can express yourself through them.

**PRONUNCIATION TIPS**

Giovanni [jo-**vahn**-nee] Paisiello [pah-ee-see-**ehl**-loh  - quickly skip through the second syllable]

# Nel cor più non mi sento

words by
Giuseppe Palomba

music by
Giovanni Paisiello

tu.  Mi piz - zi-chi, mi stuz-zi-chi, mi pun - gi - chi, mi

mas - ti - chi;  che co - sa è que - sto ahi - mè?___ pie - tà, ___ pie - tà, ___ pie -

tà! ___  a - mo - re è un cer - to che, _____ che di - spe - rar ___ mi

fa.

# Solvejg's Song

**EDVARD GRIEG** (1843-1907)

When asked to name a famous Norwegian composer, Edvard Grieg inevitably comes to mind. He stands out not only as the most famous Norwegian composer, but as one of the only Norwegian composers to have achieved an international reputation. Grieg's strong suit was a unique brand of musical nationalism. He looked to Norway's folksong heritage for the basis for many of his pieces. His work with national folk music inspired musicians throughout Europe to take a new interest in the various folk traditions of their own countries. Grieg was known as a miniaturist, primarily devoting his time to small pieces. Although his Piano Concerto is his most widely known piece, it is not typical of his work. The composer's first music lessons were with his mother. When the Norwegian violinist Ole Bull heard the fifteen-year-old Grieg play the piano in 1858, he arranged for the young musician to enter the Leipzig Conservatory in Germany, even though his parents hated to send him so far away. The young musician was unhappy at the Conservatory, but consoled himself by hearing the likes of Clara Schumann and Richard Wagner in performance. Although Grieg returned to Oslo after his studies in Germany and Denmark, his career kept him travelling throughout Europe. During his lifetime he was honored as one of his country's foremost composers and was awarded honorary degrees by both Cambridge and Oxford.

**THOUGHTS ABOUT THE SONG ...**

*Peer Gynt* is a dramatic poem in five acts by the great Norwegian playwright Henrik Ibsen, written in 1867. Grieg composed a substantial score of "incidental" theatre music for a production that took place in 1876. Some of Grieg's music for *Peer Gynt* was subsequently collected in two suites for orchestra. These have become a regular part of the international symphonic repertoire, heard around the world. The story is about Peer Gynt, a young, lazy, boastful, but charming peasant farmer. He attends the wedding of his former girlfriend, Ingrid, and there meets Solvejg. The tale then takes many turns, steeped in Nordic legend. Peer has many misadventures throughout his life. Old and broken he returns to Norway, finding truth in the redeeming love of Solvejg, who has waited for him for many, many years. In "Solvejg's Song," presented here in English translation, we hear her longing for her beloved Peer. She sadly sings of the passing of time and her promise to faithfully await his return. In the second verse she prays for Peer's safety, and wonders if he is still alive. In the "Ah" sections at the end of each verse it's as if Solvejg is attempting to cheer herself with a song. Though the music is apparently happy in this part, there is a longing and sadness just under the surface. A good performance will communicate that this is a very downhearted woman bravely trying to be hopeful and cheerful in the face of adversity and loneliness and worry. The high A's at the end of each verse needn't be pianissimo, but you should try to let them be free, easily produced, and sung as sweetly as possible.

**PRONUNCIATION TIPS**

Edvard [**ed**-vahrd] Grieg [greeg]
Henrik Ibsen [**ib**-sun - pronounce the i as in "rib"]
Solvejg [**sohl**-fehg]

# Solvejg's Song

poem by
Henrik Ibsen
English version by Arthur Westbrook

music by
Edvard Grieg

May God guide your feet, if on earth still you rove, on earth still you rove. __ His bless-ed peace be yours, if in

realms a - bove, in realms a - bove. __ Faith-ful-ly I'll bide till a - gain you draw near, a - gain you draw near, But

if you wait in heav-en, at last I'll meet you there, at last I'll meet you there!___ Ah!___

# 'Tis the Last Rose of Summer

**FRIEDRICH FLOWTOW** (Adolf Ferdinand) (1812-1883)

As the son of a wealthy, German landowner, Friedrich Flowtow was expected to enter a career in diplomacy. Instead, at sixteen, he entered the Paris Conservatory, studying both piano and composition. After returning to Germany in 1830, Flowtow saw his first opera premiered in Ludwigslust in 1835. He was 23 years old at the time. Although he later returned to Paris and lived there for several years, his aristocratic status made it difficult for him to stay following the 1848 revolution. Returning to Germany, he eventually accepted a position as a musician in the court of the Grand Duke of Schwerin. In 1863 he left Germany again, living in Austria for a time. He eventually returned to his homeland, and settled in Darmstadt, Germany. Flowtow is credited with some two dozen operas, five ballets, two piano concertos, a symphony and various songs. In his strongest works he combined the lyricism of Italian opera, the elegance of French music and the sentimental style of his native Germany. His most successful operas were *Alessandro Scarlatti*, based on stories about the Italian composer's life, and *Martha*. (*Martha* was based on a ballet which itself had been based on a vaudeville production.) Flowtow included a setting of the traditional Irish folksong "The Last Rose of Summer" (the poem is by Tom Moore) into the opera *Martha*, which is set in England in the year 1710. *Martha* was once a popular opera in the international repertoire, but in recent decades productions have become rare outside Germany.

**THOUGHTS ABOUT THE SONG ...**

This is one of the most enduring and beautiful songs in the English language. The song is a sentimental musing over a single rose, the last of the summer, left alone in the garden in the fall, while all the other roses have withered and died. The words and imagery are so lovely and so deeply felt that one can't help but feel that there is more meaning than is apparent. Like all good poetry, there are at least a couple levels of meaning in the words. It may be a mistake to create a scenario of exact meaning behind the words. However, it is very important for singers to realize that subtext is a key to a meaningful performance of most songs. Subtext means a range of emotions that is behind the words, motivating them. For example, imagine that you are asked to sing the words "get out of here." Depending on the context, the emotional subtext could be many different things, from "get out of here this minute before I hit you!," to a simple command to a tiresome cat, to a joking comment to a good friend who has said something outrageously funny. There could be many interpretations. A song as profound and indirect as "'Tis the Last Rose of Summer" needs it's own subtext. A commonly held interpretation might be that the "rose" is an aging beloved, one to whom the narrator in the poem remains ever faithful. There are other possibilities. Use your imagination. This is the essence of reading and interpreting any poem.

**PRONUNCIATION TIPS**

Friedrich [**free**-drick] Flotow [**floh**-tov]

# 'Tis the Last Rose of Summer

poem by
Tom Moore

old Irish air
setting by Friedrich Flotow
from the opera *Martha*